Edward Gregso...

Six Little Piano Pieces

Novello London

Order No: NOV 100341

To Paul and Chris Banks

SIX LITTLE PIANO PIECES

EDWARD GREGSON
(1982, rev. 1993)

1

Quite slow and precisely (♪ = 88)

A little faster (♪ = 100)

* keys to be depressed silently.

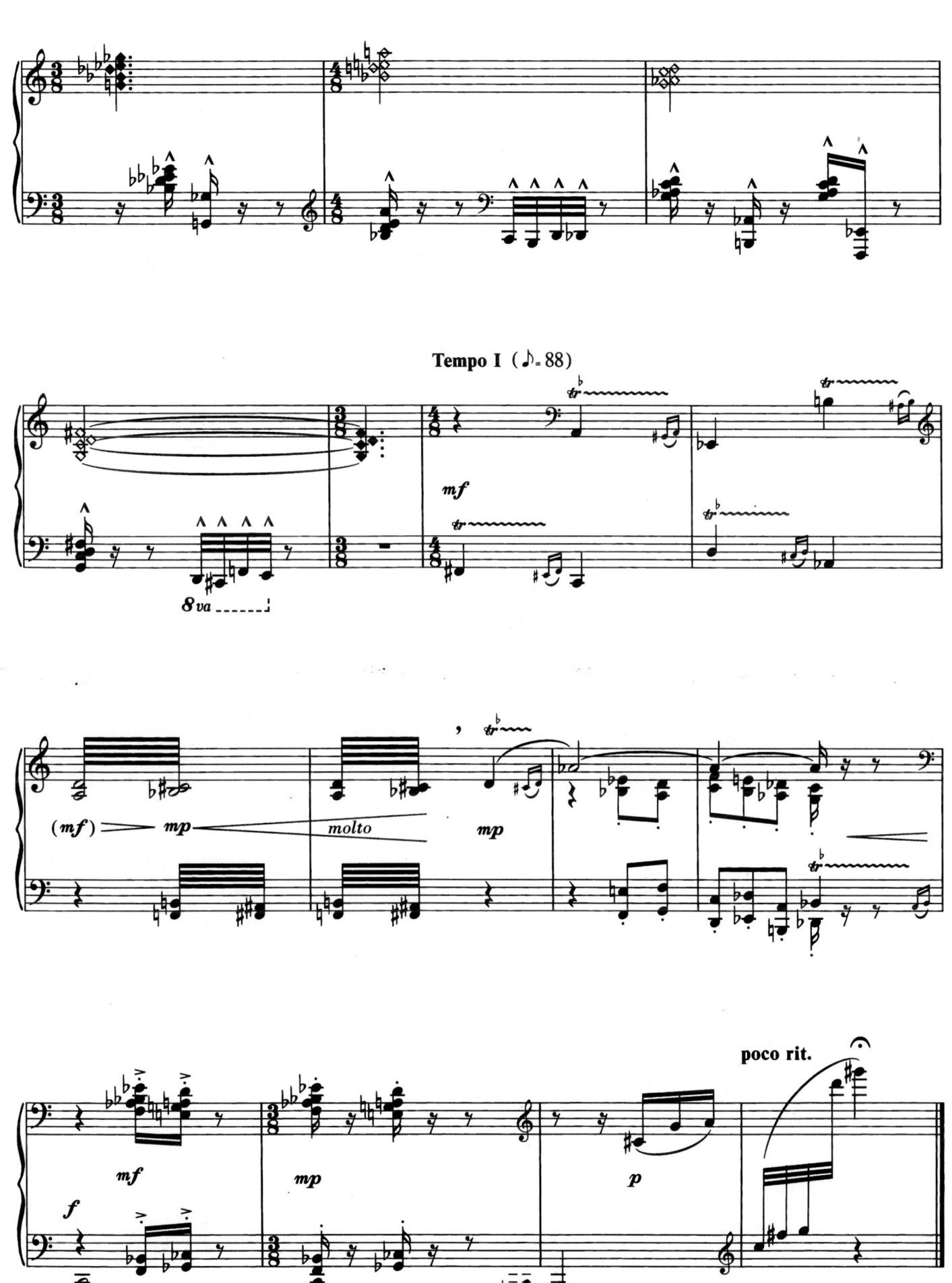

Tempo I (♪= 88)

2

Fast and playful (♩.= 88)

5

3

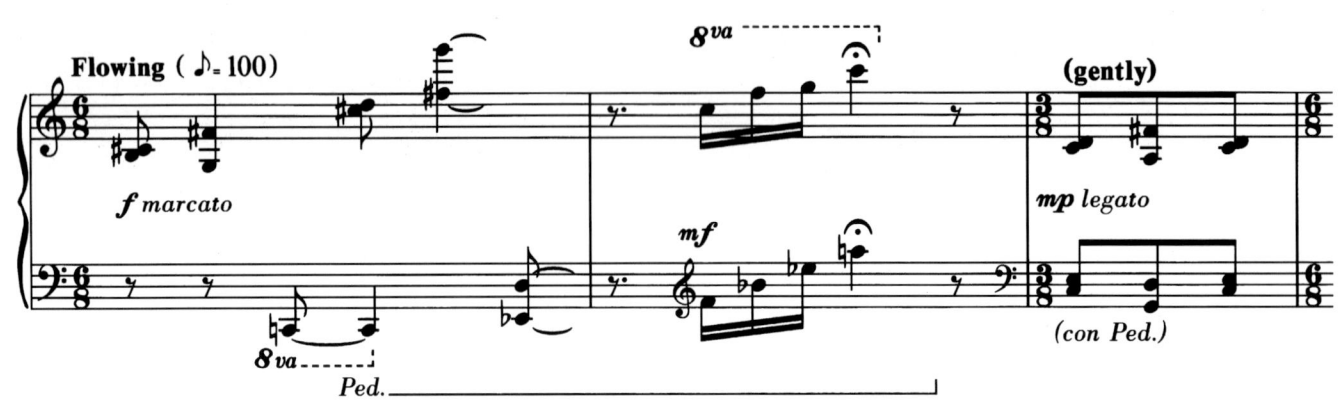

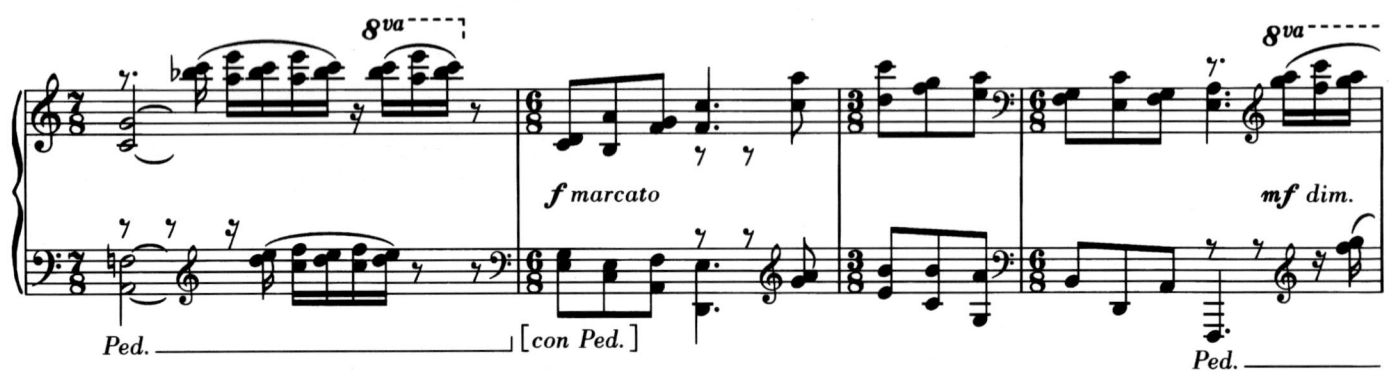

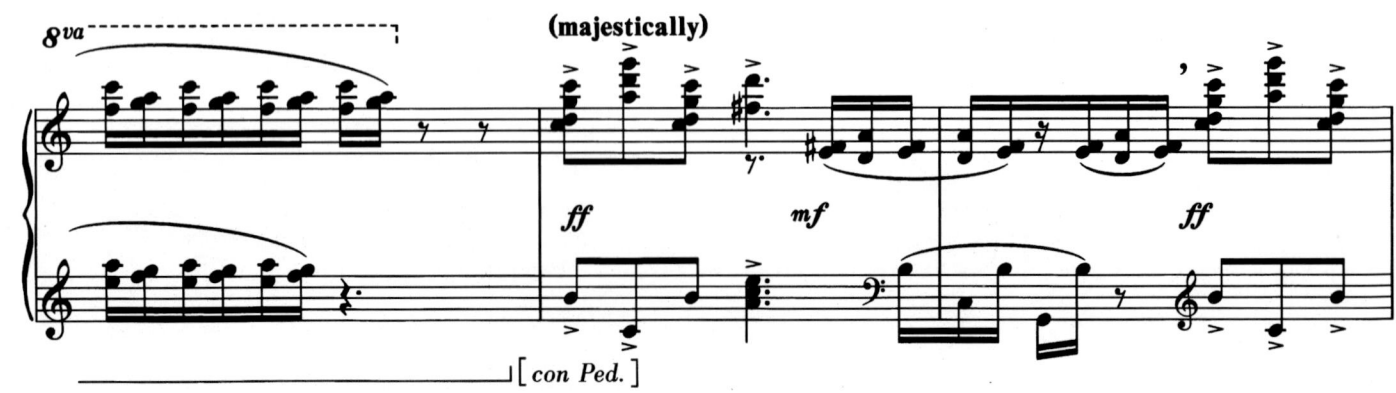

Slightly slower

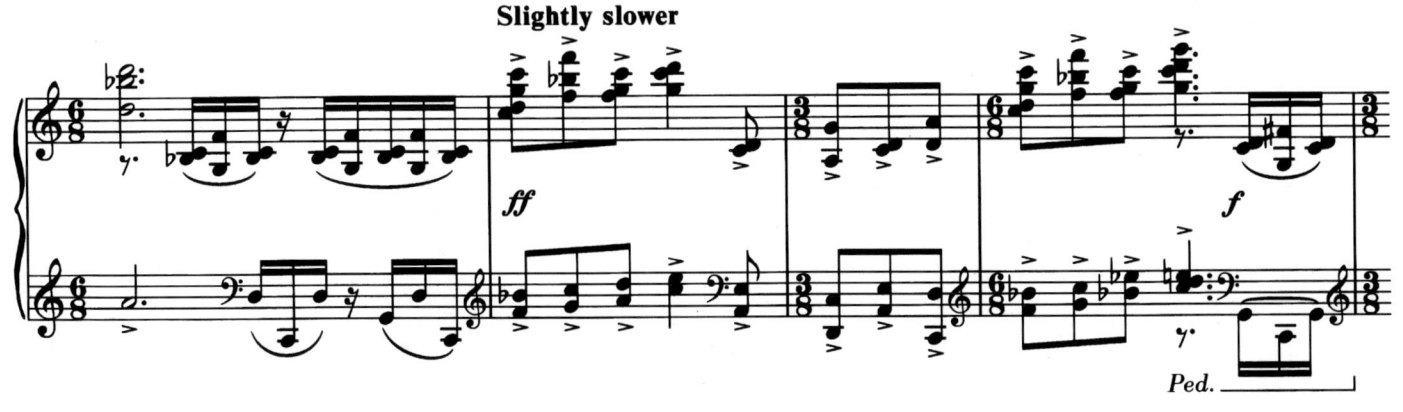

(attacca)

4

Not too fast (♩ = 100)

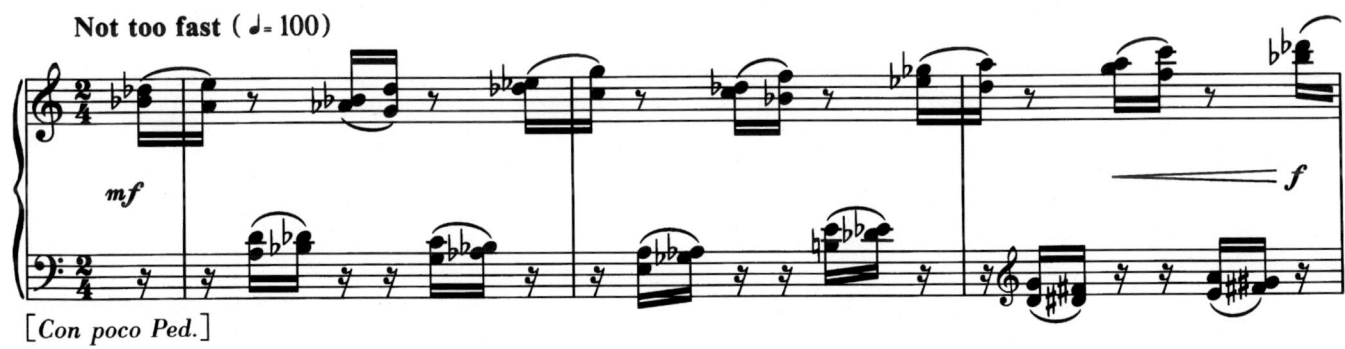

[Con poco Ped.]

5

6

With energy (♩=112)

[senza Ped.]

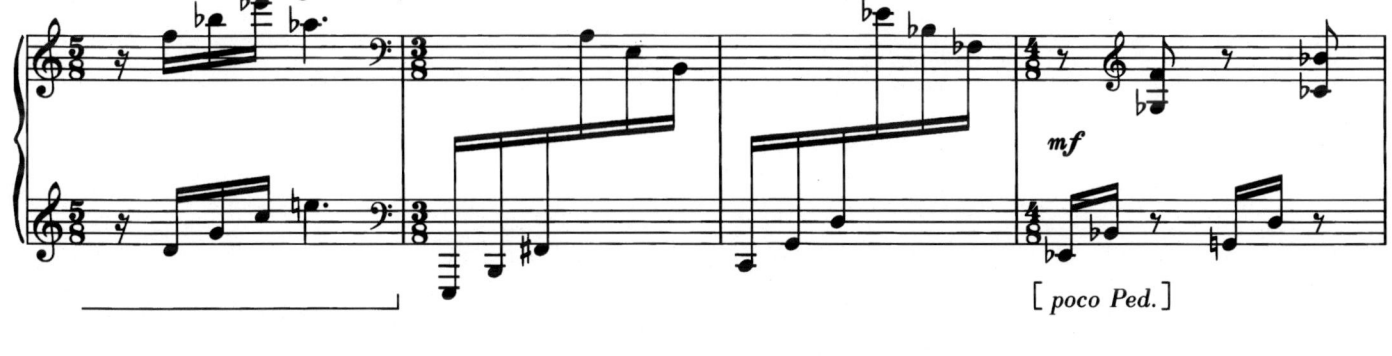

[poco Ped.]

cresc. - - - - - - f

[senza Ped.]

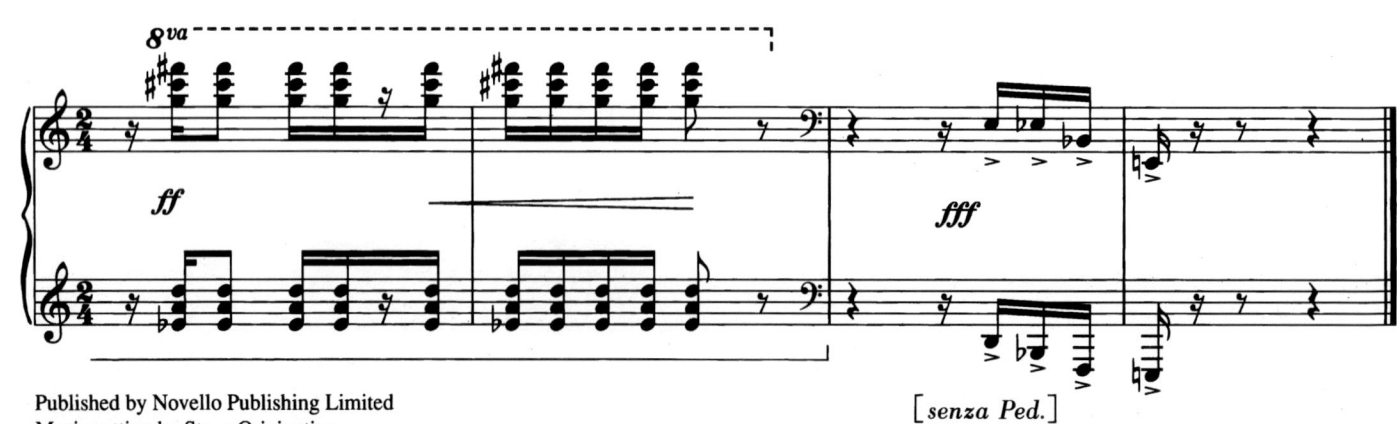

Published by Novello Publishing Limited
Music setting by Stave Origination
Printed in Great Britain

[*senza Ped.*]

2/05(53925)

SIX LITTLE PIANO PIECES

Commissioned by Richard Deering with funds provided by the Arts Council of Great Britain
and first performed by him in Amsterdam in October 1982. The pieces were revised in 1993
and are now published in this version.

Duration c. 9 minutes

Composer's note

The title *Six Little Piano Pieces* has of course been used before, most notably by
Schoenberg in his op. 19 (1911) set. Although my pieces are not in any real sense
a homage to that set, they do apply some of the same compositional procedures -
compression of form, motivic use of a limited number of pitches, a concentration
on timbre and texture and a reduction of the means of musical expression.

As with Schoenberg's set, my pieces are not 'little' in any other sense than being
relatively short. In fact two of the pieces (nos. 4 & 6) are quite extended and
technically demanding, whilst some are whimsical (no. 2) and make use of parody
(the quasi-Viennese waltz of no. 5). Two of the pieces were sketched when I was
a student, whilst others were sketches for my much larger *Piano Sonata in one*
movement which was completed in 1983. However I have tried to unify the pieces
in a number of ways - temporal relationships and the use of common material.

Finally, although I am not a Schoenbergian, it must be said that I do doff my hat
in his direction with some admiration in these pieces.

Edward Gregson
June 1995